T0060621

LAUGH
-Out-
LOUD
Springtime
JOKES
for KIDS

LAUGH
-Out-
LOUD
Springtime
JOKES
for KIDS

ROB ELLIOTT

HARPER
An Imprint of HarperCollins Publishers

Spring is a time to celebrate new life. Joanna and I were married in the spring, beginning a wonderful life together over 25 years ago. Her love, support, encouragement, and humor have kept me going.

Q: Why did the Easter egg hide?

A: Because it was a little chicken.

Q: Why did the egg go to bed?

A: Because it was fried.

Q: What do Bambi and the Easter bunny have in common?

A: They are both buck-toothed.

Q: How does the Easter bunny stay in shape?

A: He gets lots of eggs-ercise.

Q: How do pigs relax on a spring day?

A: In a ham-mock.

Q: Why did the farmer put a monkey, a giraffe, and an elephant in his garden?

A: He wanted to grow zoo-cchini.

Farmer Bob: How's your corn growing this year?

Farmer Sue: It's a-maize-ing!

Q: What is a penguin's favorite vegetable?

A: Snow peas.

Q: Why did the Easter bunny want to be a comedian?

A: He was a funny bunny.

Q: What do you get when you cross the Easter bunny and a frog?

A: Rabbit, rabbit, rabbit.

Q: Why do farmers bury their money in the ground?

A: They want to have rich soil.

Q: What did the gardener do when all her plants wilted?

A: She threw in the trowel.

Knock, knock.

Who's there?

Ears.

Ears who?

Ears hoping you have a great spring!

Q: What's the most delicious flower?

A: A delphini-yum!

Q: What kind of bug is always on time?

A: A clock-roach.

Q: **What did the Easter bunny say when he was left to color all the eggs by himself?**

A: I'm dyeing over here!

Q: **What kind of jokes do chickens tell?**

A: Egg yokes (jokes)!

Knock, knock.

Who's there?

Olive.

Olive who?

Olive springtime!

Q: Why does the Easter bunny only deliver once a year?

A: Hare today, gone tomorrow.

Q: How do you make a rabbit stew?

A: Make it wait a few hours.

Q: What is the difference between Thanksgiving and April Fools' Day?

A: One day you're thankful and the other you're prankful.

Q: Why did the robin save all its money?

A: It wanted a little nest egg someday.

Q: How did the dog know its owner was calling?

A: It had collar ID.

Q: What is a gardener's favorite game?

A: Tic-tac-grow.

Knock, knock.

Who's there?

Ada.

Ada who?

Ada bag of jelly beans and now I'm sick!

Knock, knock.

Who's there?

Phillip.

Phillip who?

Phillip my Easter basket with candy!

Q: Why did the chicken take a nap?

A: It was eggs-hausted.

Q: Why did the farmer tell jokes to his ducks?

A: He wanted to quack them up!

Knock, knock.

Who's there?

Weirdo.

Weirdo who?

Weirdo you think they hid all the Easter eggs?

Q: How does a rabbit style its fur?

A: With hare spray.

Q: What do you get when you cross a rabbit and a clam?

A: The Oyster bunny!

Q: What is a bunny's favorite kind of movie?

A: The kind with a hoppy ending.

Q: Why did the Easter bunny give eggs to everybody?

A: He doesn't want to put all his eggs in one basket.

Knock, knock.

Who's there?

Wendy.

Wendy who?

Wendy Easter bunny comes, be sure and let me know.

Knock, knock.

Who's there?

Heidi.

Heidi who?

Heidi Easter eggs in the backyard.

Q: Why don't dinosaurs celebrate Easter?

A: They're eggs-tinct!

Q: What does a duck wear to its wedding?

A: A ducks-edo!

Knock, knock.

Who's there?

Thumb.

Thumb who?

Thumbunny loves you!

Mom: Do you like your Easter basket?

Son: It's eggs-actly what I was hoping

for!

Q: What kind of fruit do you grow in a

graveyard?

A: Straw-buries.

Q: What do you get when you cross a vegetable and a pair of scissors?

A: Par-snips.

Knock, knock.

Who's there?

Robin.

Robin who?

Who's Robin all my Easter candy?

Q: What kind of pole can't you climb?

A: A tadpole.

Q: What kind of shoes do monsters wear in the rain?

A: Ghoul-oshes.

Q: Why couldn't the butterfly get into the dance?

A: Because it was a moth-ball.

Q: Why is the Easter bunny so lucky?

A: It has four rabbit's feet.

Q: Why did the Easter bunny go to the gym?

A: For its hare-obics class.

Q: Where does a rabbit eat its dinner?

A: At the vege-table.

Q: **What do you get when you combine a snake and a rabbit?**

A: A jump rope.

Q: **Which flowers make good friends?**

A: Rose-buds.

Q: **What kind of flower can't you trust?**

A: A lie-lac.

Sarah: Mom, can I plant flowers in the spring?

Mom: Yes, you May!

- - - - - - - - - - - - - - - - - - - -

Q: What is the Easter bunny's favorite game?

A: Hopscotch.

Q: What did the Easter bunny say to his girlfriend?

A: You make me so hoppy!

Q: Why did the robin get a library card?

A: It was hoping to find some bookworms.

Q: What did the rabbit say to the carrot?

A: It's been nice gnawing you.

Q: Where do rabbits go after their wedding?

A: On their bunny-moon!

Q: What kind of bugs weigh less every day?

A: Lightening bugs.

Q: Why do bunnies like math so much?

A: They're always multiplying!

Knock, knock.

Who's there?

Howard.

Howard who?

Howard you like to paint some Easter eggs?

Knock, knock.

Who's there?

Stella.

Stella who?

Stella 'nother Easter egg and I'm telling on you!

Q: Why don't chickens buy Easter eggs?

A: They're too cheep!

Q: When is the best time to jump on a trampoline?

A: In spring-time!

Q: What falls down but never gets hurt?

A: Rain-drops!

Q: Why do chickens throw great parties?

A: They're always an eggs-travaganza!

- -

Q: What is smarter than a talking bunny?

A: A spelling bee.

Q: How do you get an egg to laugh?

A: You crack it up!

Q: Why couldn't the earthworm play outside?

A: It was grounded.

Q: When do eggs wake up?

A: At the crack of dawn.

Q: What is a frog's favorite flower?

A: A croak-us.

Q: How do flowers kiss?

A: They use their tulips!

Q: Why do potatoes make good detectives?

A: They keep their eyes peeled.

Q: What does a wasp wear when it's raining?

A: A yellow jacket.

Knock, knock.

Who's there?

Owl.

Owl who?

Owl always love springtime!

Q: **Why did the berry go out with the fig?**

A: Because it couldn't get a date.

Q: Why do leprechauns make good gardeners?

A: They have green thumbs.

Q: **Why did the hen only come out in the summer, fall, and winter?**

A: She was no spring chicken!

Q: **What kind of leprechaun plays tricks on you?**

A: A lepre-con.

Q: How do bees fix their hair?

A: With a honey-comb.

Q: What goes up when the rain comes down?

A: An umbrella.

Q: What do bakers like to plant in their garden?

A: Flours.

Q: What happened when the rabbit lost his Easter candy?

A: He was hopping mad!

Q: What happened when the Easter bunny made a basket?

A: He scored two points!

Q: What monster always comes out on April 1st?

A: Prankenstein.

Q: What kind of bow can't you tie?

A: A rainbow.

Q: Why did the skunk become a police officer?

A: It believed in law and odor.

Q: **What do you call an angry vegetable?**

A: A grum-pea!

Q: **Where do trees go when they are tired?**

A: Forrest (For rest).

Q: **What kinds of birds are never happy?**

A: Bluebirds.

Q: **When is a snail the life of the party?**

A: When it comes out of its shell.

Q: **When do bees keep you healthy?**

A: When they're vitamin B's.

Q: **What is the shortest month of the year?**

A: May—it only has three letters.

Q: **Why did the snowman wear sunscreen?**

A: It didn't want to get freezer burn!

Q: **Why did the farmer take his cows to the gym?**

A: To build up their moo-scles.

Knock, knock.

Who's there?

Carrie.

Carrie who?

Carrie my Easter basket for me?

Q: What happened when the farmer lost his pig?

A: He tractor down.

Q: Why did the boy push the egg down the hill?

A: He wanted an egg roll.

Q: What do you get when you cross a mad sheep with an angry cow?

A: You get an animal in a very baaaaaaad moooood!

Q: Why are gardeners never lonely?

A: They have a lot of buds.

Q: Why did the farmer go to school?

A: She wanted to go on a field trip.

Q: Why did the pig get sent to his room?

A: It told a dirty joke.

Farmer: Why aren't my radishes growing?

Farmer's wife: Beets me!

Q: What do you get when you cross a cow and a superhero?

A: Something legen-dairy!

Q: What does the Easter bunny eat when it's hot outside?

A: Hop-sicles.

Q: Why wouldn't the farmer go in the cornfield?

A: He was afraid of being stalked.

Q: Why do seeds make great friends?

A: They're always rooting for you!

Knock, knock.

Who's there?

Turnip.

Turnip who?

Turnip the heat—I'm freezing!

Q: What kind of vegetable is hot and cold at the same time?

A: A chilly pepper.

- -

Knock, kock.

Who's there?

Hominy.

Hominy who?

Hominy Easter eggs did you find?

Joe: Your pig needs a bath.

John: Hogwash!

Q: How did the farmer fix his

overalls?

A: With a cabbage patch.

Q: Why did the farmer hire a baker?

A: He wanted to rake in the dough!

Q: Why did the bee go to the allergist?

A: It had hives.

Q: How does a boy let you know he called?

A: He leaves a voice male.

Q: Why did the farmer bring a saddle to the garden?

A: He was growing horse-radish.

Q: Why are dogs such great gardeners?

A: They use a lot of fur-tilizer.

Q: Why is the Easter bunny such a good listener?

A: Because he's all ears!

Q: What did Humpty Dumpty study in school?

A: Egg-onomics.

Q: Why couldn't the Easter bunny go to the party?

A: He was up to his ears in work.

Q: Why did the egg have to get a job?

A: Because he was broke!

Q: Why can't a scarecrow be a comedian?

A: Its jokes are too corny.

Q: What is a plumber's favorite vegetable?

A: A leek!

Q: What do you get when you combine a pig and a cow?

A: A ham-burger.

Q: What do you call a bunny who studies philosophy?

A: Eggs-istential.

Knock, knock.

Who's there?

Navy bean.

Navy bean who?

I've navy bean so glad to see you!

Q: What do pandas eat in the spring?

A: Straw-bearies.

Q: Why was the strawberry stressed

out?

A: It was in a jam!

Knock, knock.

Who's there?

Peas.

Peas who?

Peas and thank you are good manners.

Q: Why did the grape go to bed?

A: It ran out of juice!

Q: Why do melons stay single?

A: Because they cantaloupe.

Q: What don't grizzlies wear shoes?

A: They like to go bear-foot.

Q: Why did the cucumber call for help?

A: It was in a pickle.

Q: What happens to snowmen in April?

A: They have a meltdown!

Knock, knock.

Who's there?

Pudding.

Pudding who?

I'm pudding chocolate in your Easter basket.

Knock, knock.

Who's there?

Tommy.

Tommy who?

My tommy hurts from too much Easter candy.

Q: What happened when the gardener saw a monster?

A: She wet her plants.

Q: When do the monkeys come out at the zoo?

A: In Ape-ril.

Q: Why did the mop marry the broom?

A: It was swept off its feet.

Q: How do you fix a broken vegetable?

A: With tomato paste.

Q: Why did the apple go to the gym?

A: To work on its core.

Q: What do you get when you combine an apple and a tree?

A: A pine-apple.

Q: Why did the Easter bunny collapse on April 1st?

A: It just finished a thirty-one-day March!

Q: Who borrows your Rollerblades all the time?

A: A cheap-skate!

Q: What do mallards watch on TV?

A: Duck-umentaries.

Q: Why was the Easter bunny at the top of his class?

A: He was an egghead.

Joel: Did you hear the joke about the strawberry jam?

Jill: Yes, it's spreading all over the place!

Q: Why was the mushroom invited to all the spring parties?

A: Because he was such a fun-gi.

Q: What did the robin do when it got sick?

A: It went to the doctor for tweetment.

Knock, knock.

Who's there?

Pasture.

Pasture who?

It's pasture bedtime—go to sleep!

Q: What do you get when you cross a cow and a zucchini?

A: A vegeta-bull.

Q: What do you call a sheep that does karate?

A: A lamb chop.

Q: Why are flowers so lazy?

A: They're always in their beds.

Knock, knock.

Who's there?

Kenneth.

Kenneth who?

Kenneth be my turn to find Easter eggs?

Q: What did the egg say to the circus clown?

A: You crack me up!

Q: Why did the cow cross the pasture?

A: To get to the udder side.

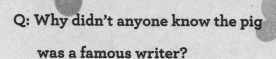

Q: Why didn't anyone know the pig was a famous writer?

A: Because he used a pen name.

Q: What do you call a tuna in space?

A: A starfish.

Q: Why do cats like spring?

A: The weather is purr-fect.

Q: Why did the bug hide its trophies in the closet?

A: It was a humble bee.

Q: What is a cat's favorite vegetable?

A: As-purr-agus.

Q: How do spiders like their corn?

A: On the cobweb.

Q: What can you serve but never eat?

A: A tennis ball.

Q: What do you get when you cross Bambi and an umbrella?

A: A rain-deer.

Q: Why was the insect so polite?

A: Because it was a ladybug.

Q: What do you call a forest full of zombies?

A: Petrified wood!

Q: Why are chickens so bad at baseball?

A: They're always hitting fowl balls.

Q: What kind of birds end up in jail?

A: Rob-ins!

Q: What do you get when you cross a volcano and a vegetable?

A: A lava-cado!

Q: When is a pig a tattletale?

A: When it squeals on you.

Knock, knock.

Who's there?

Doughnut.

Doughnut who?

Doughnut love shoveling snow, so I love spring!

Q: What is the Easter bunny's favorite kind of music?

A: Hip-hop.

Q: Why did the crow pick up the phone?

A: To caw, caw, caw somebody!

Q: Why don't you ever see elephants hiding in trees?

A: Because they're so good at it.

Q: Why are frogs always happy?

A: They eat what bugs them.

Q: How do you get a farmer on a spaceship?

A: You use a tractor beam.

Q: Why did the chicken go skydiving?

A: It wanted to try eggs-treme sports.

Q: Why did the pig put on suntan lotion?

A: It didn't want to bacon the sun.

Q: Why did the sponge go south for spring break?

A: It wanted to soak up the sun!

Q: Why did the caterpillar go to so many parties?

A: It was a social butterfly.

Q: Why did the soccer player drop out of school?

A: He didn't have any goals.

Knock, knock.

Who's there?

Noah.

Noah who?

Noah-body. April fools!

Knock, knock.

Who's there?

Petunia.

Petunia who?

Petunia shoes and come out and play!

Q: What's a giraffe's favorite fruit?

A: A neck-tarine.

Knock, knock.

Who's there?

Checker.

Checker who?

Checker basket to see if you find any candy.

Knock, knock.

Who's there?

Baby owl.

Baby owl who?

Baby, owl see you after spring break.

Q: What kind of vegetable gets a pedicure?

A: A toma-toe.

Q: How do you get your Easter egg to shrink?

A: You put it on a dye-it.

Q: What happens if you tell an Easter egg a joke?

A: It will dye laughing!

Sam: What are you planting in your garden this year?

Jack: Beets me!

Q: What do you get when you cross a fruit with a rock?

A: A pome-granite.

Q: What vegetable doesn't have any manners?

A: A rude-abaga.

Q: What kind of bug never stops complaining?

A: A grumble bee.

Q: What kind of vegetable plays the drums?

A: The beet!

Q: What kind of candy will give you a rash?

A: Licor-itch.

Q: What kind of candy do you put in a skunk's Easter basket?

A: Smelly beans.

Q: What do you get if you cross candy and balloons?

A: Lolli-pops!

Q: Why wouldn't the lobster share its Easter candy?

A: It's shellfish!

Q: **What did the Easter bunny say when it was time to go?**

A: Let's bounce.

Q: **What do you put in Santa's Easter basket?**

A: Jolly beans.

Q: **Why did the lemon marry the lime?**

A: It was his main squeeze.

Q: **What do you call a snowman on spring break?**

A: A puddle.

Q: Why couldn't the girl get anything to grow in her garden?

A: She didn't know beans about it.

Q: What do you call a cabbage on a plane?

A: A vegetable with its head in the clouds.

Q: What is the most adorable kind of bug?

A: A cuter-pillar.

Knock, knock.

Who's there?

Wayne.

Wayne who?

Wayne will help the flowers grow.

Knock, knock.

Who's there?

Norma Lee.

Norma Lee who?

Norma Lee I like to play outside in the rain.

Q: What is orange and sounds like a parrot?

A: A carrot.

Q: Why don't pigs like spring?

A: They think it's a boar!

Q: What kind of mint is bad to eat?

A: A var-mint.

Q: Where do hunters like to shop?

A: Target.

Q: Why did the Easter bunny stay home?

A: He was having a bad hare day.

Q: Why was the chocolate bunny sad?

A: It felt hollow inside.

Q: What do bugs write on?

A: Flypaper.

Q: What do you call a wasp that doesn't cost anything?

A: A free-bee.

Q: When do fish swim away and hide?

A: On Fry-days!

Patrick: Who can help me find a four-leaf clover?

Shannon: A lepre-can!

Q: **What kind of animal doesn't have a name?**

A: The anony-moose.

Q: **What is a gardener's favorite drink?**

A: Root beer.

Q: **What did the skunk pay for its Easter candy?**

A: One scent!

Q: **What happened when the Easter bunny lost all the eggs?**

A: It was a basket case.

- - - - - - - - - - - - - - - - - - - -

Q: What do you call a scarecrow that follows you everywhere you go?

A: A corn stalker!

Q: What do you get when you cross a dog and a bug?

A: A butter-flea!

Q: What did summer say to spring?

A: Help, I'm going to fall!

Lisa: Does your dog like its flea collar?

Anna: No, he's ticked off!

Q: What do rabbits wear in the cafeteria?

A: A hare-net.

Q: What is a cowboy's favorite plant?

A: A rodeo-dendron.

Q: Why did the Easter bunny hide under the bed?

A: So he could be a dust bunny.

Knock, knock.

Who's there?

Gopher.

Gopher who?

Gopher the ball and you might catch it!

Q: What do you get when you cross a cricket and a lawn mower?

A: A grasshopper!

Q: Why did the girl play her drum outside?

A: She wanted to beat around the bush.

Q: What do leprechauns eat for breakfast?

A: Lucky Charms.

Q: Why were the golfers eating sandwiches and cake?

A: They were having a tee party.

Knock, knock.

Who's there?

Bunny.

Bunny who?

Some bunny ate all my Easter candy!

Knock, knock.

Who's there?

Arthur.

Arthur who?

Arthur any more chocolate Easter bunnies?

Q: How does Easter end?

A: With an "r."

Q: What do you get if you give a robin a paintbrush?

A: A picture that's worth a thousand worms.

Q: Why did the duck and the chicken get fired?

A: They kept cracking yokes on the job.

Q: Why did the pig get kicked off the farm?

A: He was dis*grunt*led!

Q: How do you stop a dog in its tracks?

A: Hit the paws button.

Q: What did the meteorologist do when she broke her leg?

A: She put it in a fore-cast.

Q: Why can't you win a race with a lettuce?

A: They always have a head start.

Q: Why was the little bean crying?

A: It wanted its eda-mommy.

Q: What does a snake like to wear?

A: Ser-pants!

Q: What kind of stone isn't hard?

A: A sham-rock!

Knock, knock.

Who's there?

Glove.

Glove who?

Glove to hang out with you in springtime.

Q: How do you take a pig to the hospital?

A: In a ham-bulance.

Q: Why was the robin eating cake?

A: It was its bird-thday.

Q: What is the Easter bunny's favorite sport?

A: Basket-ball.

Q: What is a mallard's favorite game?

A: Duck, duck, goose.

Q: Where do pigs like to go for spring break?

A: New Ham-pshire.

Q: What do you get when you combine the Easter bunny and a bumblebee?

A: A honey bunny.

Q: What do rabbits use to style their hair?

A: A hare dryer.

Q: What does the Easter bunny like to plant in the garden?

A: Eggplants.

Q: How does the Easter bunny like to travel?

A: By hare-plane.

Q: What kind of batteries should you bury?

A: Dead ones.

Knock, knock.

Who's there?

Darrell.

Darrell who?

Darrell be a fun Easter egg hunt this afternoon!

Q: What kind of bears come out in the spring?

A: Drizzly bears.

Q: How do skunks go sightseeing?

A: In a smell-icopter.

Q: How did the T. rex feel after soccer practice?

A: Dino-sore.

Q: Why did the banana join the gymnastics team?

A: It wanted to do the splits.

Q: What is a tree's favorite vegetable?

A: Oak-ra.

Q: **Why did the spider leave candy wrappers all over the ground?**

A: It was a litter-bug.

George: I ate too many hamburgers for dinner.

Henry: That was a big mis-steak!

Knock, knock.

Who's there?

Jello.

Jello who?

Jello, come out and play with me!

Q: **What do bunnies do the day after Easter?**

A: They let their hare down.

Q: **Why did the Easter bunny call in sick?**

A: He had spring fever.

Q: **What do you get when you cross a spider and a computer?**

A: A web-site!

Q: **What did Frosty do when he met the Easter bunny?**

A: He gave him the cold shoulder.

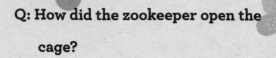

Q: How did the zookeeper open the cage?

A: With a mon-key.

Q: When do they party in the castle?

A: All knight long!

Q: Where do gardeners sleep?

A: In flower beds.

Q: Where does a peach take a nap?

A: In an apri-cot.

Q: What do you call an egg on April Fools' Day?

A: A practical yolker!

Q: What do you get when you combine a fish and a camel?

A: A humpback whale.

Q: What is a kangaroo's favorite season?

A: Spring.

Q: What do you get when you cross a kitten and a bulldozer?

A: A bob-cat.

Q: Why did the Easter bunny stay in bed?

A: He was going undercover.

Knock, knock.

Who's there?

Sherwood.

Sherwood who?

Sherwood be nice if you came along

on our egg hunt.

Knock, knock.

Who's there?

Juicy.

Juicy who?

Juicy where the Easter eggs are

hidden?

Q: **What happened to the chicken who broke all the rules at school?**

A: It got eggs-spelled.

Knock, knock.

Who's there?

Ice cream.

Ice cream who?

Ice cream for springtime!

Knock, knock.

Who's there?

Diesel.

Diesel who?

Diesel be another great Easter, I'm sure!

Q: Where do writers go for spring break?

A: Pencil-vania.

Q: Why did the Easter bunny put his radio in the freezer?

A: He wanted some cool music.

Q: What's a bunny's favorite restaurant?

A: IHOP.

Q: What do you call a rabbit at a hotel?

A: A bell-hop.

Sam: How do we know carrots are good for our eyes?

Emma: Have you ever seen a rabbit with glasses?

Q: How does a farmer write a letter?

A: With a pig-pen.

Q: When does a snake make you laugh?

A: When it's hiss-terical.

Q: What do you get when you cross a flower and a merry-go-round?

A: A dizzy daisy.

Q: What do rabbits buy at the bakery?

A: Hot cross bun-nies.

Q: What do you call a zombie in the garden?

A: Grow-tesque.

Q: What kind of shoes do frogs wear to the beach?

A: Open-toad shoes.

Knock, knock.

Who's there?

Howie.

Howie who?

Howie going to find all the Easter eggs?

Knock, knock.

Who's there?

Cargo.

Cargo who?

Bunny go hop, cargo vroom!

Q: Why is the baker so lazy?

A: He's always loaf-ing around.

Q: Why did the chickens stay in the coop all day?

A: Because of fowl weather.

Q: What did the alien say to the gardener?

A: Take me to your weeder.

Q: Why did the farmer throw seeds in the pool?

A: He wanted to grow water-melon.

Q: What do baseball players and foxes have in common?

A: One catches fouls and the other catches fowls.

Q: Why did the owl become a comedian?

A: Everyone said he was a hoot!

Q: Why did quarters start falling from the sky?

A: There was change in the weather.

Q: What do you get when you cross a soda and a radio?

A: Pop music!

Q: What happened to the snowman when spring came?

A: It lost its cool.

Q: Why was everybody laughing at the mountain?

A: Because it was hill-arious.

Knock, knock.

Who's there?

Everest.

Everest who?

Everest in a hammock on a spring day?

Q: How can you see your garden in the dark?

A: Plant a lot of bulbs!

Jim: It's raining cats and dogs!

Alex: April showers bring May flowers.

Jim: Yeah, but now there are poodles everywhere!

Q: What did the bunny say to the flea?

A: Quit bugging me!

Q: Why did the snail take a nap in the garden?

A: It was feeling slug-gish.

Q: What does the Easter bunny order when he's getting takeout?

A: Hop suey.

Q: What is a frog's favorite breakfast?

A: Toad-st and jam.

Knock, knock.

Who's there?

Wanda.

Wanda who?

Wanda come outside and play with me?

Q: Where do heroes buy their food?

A: The super-market!

Q: What do you get when you cross a flower and a pickle?

A: A daffo-dill.

Q: What do you get when you cross a bike and a flower?

A: Petals that pedal.

Knock, knock.

Who's there?

Justin.

Justin who?

You're Justin time for the Easter egg hunt!

Q: Why was the cat afraid of the tree?

A: It was a dogwood.

Knock, knock.

Who's there?

Juno.

Juno who?

Juno where to go for spring break?

Q: What's a lawn mower's favorite music?

A: Bluegrass!

Knock, knock.

Who's there?

Oscar.

Oscar who?

Oscar silly question, you get a silly answer.

Q: Why did the boy throw branches in the lake?

A: He wanted fish sticks.

Q: What do you get when you cross a dog and a cow?

A: Hound beef.

Q: Why did the gardener take her flower to the dentist?

A: It needed a root canal.

Q: What do you call a chicken from another planet?

A: An eggs-traterrestrial.

Knock, knock.

Who's there?

Cashew.

Cashew who?

Bless you! Do you have spring allergies?

Knock, knock.

Who's there?

Avenue.

Avenue who?

Avenue been getting ready for Easter?

Q: What has a head and a foot but no arms?

A: Your bed.

Q: Where do crayons go for spring break?

A: Color-ado.

- - - - - - - - - - - - - - - - - -

Q: **Where does a T. rex like to go on spring break?**

A: To the dino-shore.

Q: **What is a monkey's favorite cookie?**

A: Chocolate chimp.

Q: **What do you get when you cross a turtle and a porcupine?**

A: A slow-poke.

Q: **Why did the hot-air balloon get grounded?**

A: It was getting carried away.

Knock, knock.

Who's there?

Kent.

Kent who?

Kent we dye our Easter eggs now?

Knock, knock.

Who's there?

Amish.

Amish who?

Amish the spring flowers after a long winter.

Q: Why did the farmer have to patch his overalls?

A: Because you rip what you sew.

Knock, knock.

Who's there?

Police.

Police who?

Police help me weed the garden.

Q: What did the Dalmatian say after Easter dinner?

A: That hit the spot!

Knock, knock.

Who's there?

Yeast.

Yeast who?

At yeast I have an umbrella if it rains.

Knock, knock.

Who's there?

Dishes.

Dishes who?

Dishes the best Easter I've ever had.

Knock, knock.

Who's there?

Gwen.

Gwen who?

Gwen will the flowers start blooming?

Q: Why did the elephant quit the circus?

A: He was working for peanuts.

Patient: Doctor, I think I'm a chicken.

Doctor: How long have you felt like this?

Patient: Since I was an egg.

Knock, knock.

Who's there?

Iguana.

Iguana who?

Iguana go on the Easter egg hunt with you!

Knock, knock.

Who's there?

Irish.

Irish who?

Irish it was spring all year long!

Q: What do sharks like to eat for breakfast?

A: Muf-fins.

Q: What happened when the bunny dreamed he was a muffler?

A: He woke up exhausted.

Q: What do baby kittens wear?

A: Dia-purrs.

Q: What does a farmer like to wear?

A: A har-vest.

Q: What do you get when you cross a horse and an angel?

A: A hay-lo.

Q: What is the smartest kind of bug?

A: A brilli-ant.

Knock, knock.

Who's there?

Russian.

Russian who?

I'm Russian to find all my Easter eggs.

Knock, knock.

Who's there?

Hugo.

Hugo who?

Hugo that way and I'll go this way.

Knock, knock.

Who's there?

Window.

Window who?

Window we start packing for spring break?

Q: What does a golfer eat for lunch?

A: A club sandwich.

Q: What kind of vegetable has four legs and barks?

A: A collie-flower.

Q: Why does the queen always hold an umbrella?

A: Because she reigns.

Q: Why is everybody running around?

A: They're part of the human race.

Q: What did the beach say to the wave?

A: Long tide no sea!

Knock, knock.

Who's there?

Atlas.

Atlas who?

Atlas spring is here!

Q: What did the farmer give his cows for lunch?

A: Peanut udder and jelly sandwiches.

Q: How do you know if a joke is about your mom and dad?

A: When the punch line becomes a-parent!

Q: Why did the cat smell so good?

A: It was wearing purr-fume.

Q: Why are tailors so funny?

A: They always have people in stitches.

Customer: Waiter, do you serve rabbit here?

Waiter: Yes, we're happy to serve anyone.

Q: Why did the bucket go to the doctor?

A: It was looking a little pail.

Q: Why was the toad stressed out?

A: It was a worry-wart.

Q: Why did the Easter bunny give away so many baskets?

A: He was feeling eggs-travagant.

Q: Why did the Easter bunny visit the antique store?

A: He wanted to find a hare-loom.

Q: What do daylight savings and a rabbit have in common?

A: They both spring forward.

Q: How do you help out a baker?

A: Make a dough-nation.

Knock, knock.

Who's there?

Taco.

Taco who?

Taco 'bout what you'd like to do for spring break.

Q: Why did Humpty Dumpty fall off the wall?

A: Because he was an egghead.

Q: Why did the polar bear visit friends for spring break?

A: He had been feeling ice-olated.

Q: Why are chickens so hard to get along with?

A: You're always walking on eggshells around them.

Q: Why does the Easter bunny only work one day per year?

A: He puts all his eggs in one basket.

Q: Why did the Easter bunny get in a fight?

A: The chickens were egging him on.

Q: Where does the Easter bunny stay on vacation?

A: At a hare B&B.

Knock, knock.

Who's there?

Walter.

Walter who?

Walter we put in our Easter baskets this year?

Q: Why did the Easter bunny keep a dictionary in his pocket?

A: He wanted to be a smarty-pants.

Q: Why did the farmer visit the chicken coop?

A: He wanted to hang out with his peeps!

Tammy: Should we skip the chocolate bunnies for Easter this year?

Marley: No, that's a hare-brained idea!

Q: Why did the chickens need a doctor?

A: Because they flu the coop.

Q: What do you get when you cross a chicken and a clock?

A: Egg on your face.

Q: **Where did the pitcher dance with his girlfriend?**

A: At the base-ball.

Q: **Why did the vegetable have to go to bed early?**

A: It was just a little sprout.

Q: **Why did the candy salesman put his phone in the freezer?**

A: He had to make a few cold calls.

Q: **What did the oak tree say when it sprouted leaves in the spring?**

A: That's a re-leaf!

Q: **What do you get when you cross a chicken and an astronaut?**

A: A space eggs-plorer.

Q: **Why did the Easter bunny get a surfboard?**

A: He wanted to make some waves.

Q: **Why did the Easter bunny put a banana in his basket?**

A: He thought it was a-peeling.

Q: **What do you give a dog for Easter breakfast?**

A: Pupcakes and woofles.

Knock, knock.

Who's there?

Iva.

Iva who?

Iva been waiting for spring for a long time!

Q: Why did the Easter bunny put a fishing pole in his basket?

A: He was fishing for compliments.

Q: Who brings water to the baseball game?

A: The pitcher.

Q: When can't you open the refrigerator door?

A: When the salad is dressing!

Q: How did the dog feel in the spring?

A: Like he got a new leash on life.

Q: How did the cat get the bread?

A: It baked it from scratch.

Q: Why did the comedian go to Easter dinner?

A: He wanted to ham it up.

Q: How did the fish pay for his Easter candy?

A: With a credit cod.

Q: Why did the baby snake cry?

A: Someone took away its rattle.

Q: Why can't chickens play baseball?

A: They always hit fowl balls.

Q: Why was the Easter bunny in a jam?

A: He ran out of jelly beans!

Q: What do you do with a baby cow?

A: Give it a cud-dle.

Q: What do you get when you cross a frog and a clown?

A: A silly pad!

Q: Why did the softball player save all her money?

A: She was a penny pitcher!

Q: What do you call a cowboy who's glad it's spring?

A. A jolly rancher.

Q: What do fishermen eat for breakfast?

A: Boat-meal.

Q: **Where does a farmer sit when he's tired?**

A: On his cow-ch.

Q: **Why did the coffee bean stay home?**

A: It was grounded.

Q: **Why won't the Easter bunny go down the chimney?**

A: He doesn't want to catch the flue.

Q: **Where does the Easter bunny keep the eggs?**

A: In the oval office.

Q: Why can't the Easter bunny work for the tooth fairy?

A: Because a basket won't fit under your pillow!

Q: Why did the camel decide to take up baseball?

A: So it could be a hump-ire.

Ella: Mom, have you ever watched the movie *Bambi*?

Mom: Yes, deer.

Q: What does a banana peel wear to Easter dinner?

A: Slip-pers.

Q: Where do flowers go to school?

A: Kinder-garden!

Knock, knock.

Who's there?

Whisker.

Whisker who?

Whisker eggs in a mixing bowl.

Q: Why did the chicken marry a caterpillar?

A: Because chicks dig worms.

Knock, knock.

Who's there?

Canoe.

Canoe who?

Canoe help me find my Easter basket?

**Q: How does the Easter bunny deliver
so many eggs?**

A: He hops to it!

**Molly: Help, help, I'm dropping my
Easter basket!**

Mandy: Get a grip!

Q: Why does grass have such low self-esteem?

A: It's always getting cut down.

Q: Why did the referee jump in a puddle?

A: He wanted to wet his whistle.

Sam: Why did you bring your baseball bat to school?

Cam: It's time to hit the books!

<u>Tongue Twisters</u>

Brown bunnies build big baskets.

Sneaky snakes sing silly songs.

Farmers find fake fruit.

Spring, sprang, sprung.

Go, grow, glow!

Eat Easter eggs every evening.

Daffodils, daisies, dandelions.

Chew chocolate cherries.

Fresh flowers.